RAG RUGS
OLD INTO NEW
Book 1

by
Debbie Siniska

D·H·G·M·B

First published in Great Britain 2010
by D.H.G.M.Ball
Glyndale, St.Mary's Lane
Ticehurst, East Sussex
England, TN5 7AX

For my mum, Hattie Bydawell

Contents

Introduction

Recycling old woollies and tee shirts is a great way to make something new from something old. There is a wealth of readily available fabrics to be found in charity shops, car boot and jumble sales, and sourcing textiles in this way is an easy and thrifty way to get your basic materials for rag rug making. This tactile and practical art has captivated me over the past 20 years and by choosing colours and textures that attract you in the first place your artistic self-expression will have already begun to work for you.

There are many ways you can make a homely statement and express your feelings for colour with a hand hooked or proggy rag rug. From a threshold mat to welcome your visitors, to a fireside rug to keep the sparks from burning your floor, this enduring thrift craft has survived the span of time and is as relevant today as it was in the early 1900's, when it was very much a communal activity.

The personal expression that can be worked into your rag rug is infinite. Working with simple hand tools and scraps of ready to hand reclaimed textiles is fun and comes with a sense of achievement.

Oak Leaf Rug

Pink Floral Hooky Mat from the early 1900's

Humble Beginnings - A Brief History

The history of floor coverings stretches back through the centuries across all cultures. In many parts of the world, people have created sand paintings, and other markings on the ground intended to beautify, as a symbolic welcome for guests or as a magical defence, and examples of this sort of art can still be found in rural India. Floor coverings intended to make a home more comfortable are just as common – we can readily imagine that stone age people would have spread animal skins and dried grasses on the floors of their dwellings, and floor coverings such as Japanese tatami mats (woven from rice straw with a rush covering) are still common.

Rag Rugs combine both of these traditions – they are both practical floor coverings that will make a floor more comfortable (a step up from a cold stone floor!)

and in many cases they are also small works of art, with welcoming or celebratory images.

The craft has been around for hundreds of years but very few rag rugs have survived as they were used until they wore out, and because of their utilitarian use, were not considered precious or worth saving.

Mat made in 1897 to commemorate Queen Victoria's Diamond Jubilee

There is evidence that a pulled up looped pile was used 3000 years ago in ancient Egypt, perhaps as a form of embroidery that left a raised looped surface and there are examples of hooked textiles from Northern Europe dating back to the Bronze Age.

Early Scandinavian settlers to the North of England hooked wool and rag strips through a backing cloth, to make rugs and protective coverings, known as ryer (rhye in Anglo Saxon) rugs to replace animal skins. The earliest known British example dates back to around 1815/1840; this early surviving rug was made from uniforms worn at the Battle of Waterloo.

There was a strong mat making tradition on the Shetland Islands and these mats would have made up part of a brides dowry. The Shetland Islands were owned

Mat making during the 1892 Miners Strike

7

by Norway until the 15th century, linking the two country's cultures. It is likely that this route represents one of the ways in which the craft was introduced into Northern Britain.

1920's rug from the room of John Maynard Keynes at Charleston, home of the Bloomsbury group in Sussex.

It seems reasonable to suggest the European settlers in North America brought these techniques with them. There are early American examples of patchwork quilts made from worn-out clothing, and coiled braids formed into flat mats. There are also examples of hooked and proddy rugs from the USA and Canada dating from the mid 1800's, that resemble those made in the North of England.

Rag rugs would have traditionally been worked on a woven backing of coarse linen, with drawn threads to create a more open weave. In the 1830's when inexpensive hessian sackcloth (made from the jute plant) came to England from India, this became the backing of choice.

'Mixy' Hearth Mat

In the industrial communities of northern England in the late 1800's and early 1900's, rag mats were made out of necessity. People would have used their old worn out clothes worked onto a grain sack, marking out a design with a charred stick from the fire. Some sack manufacturers printed figurative designs, typically farmyard animals on their sacks, and these were often used as the basis for a rag mat design. Traditionally, rag mats would have had a dark border, and sometimes dinner plates or templates passed down through the family would have been used to create a design.

Mat making in Co. Durham 1937

In many households, all the family would have been involved in making the next rag mat for the house. Old garments would of course hold memories, and jumpers, trousers, socks and coats, blankets, Lisle stockings and flannel petticoats were all usable materials for making a family mat. Primitive tools would have been made out of old bones, keys, sticks and clothes pegs, and pretty much anything to hand.

There are many traditional names for the various types of rag rug, regional names include clippy, proddy, clootie, hooky, proggy, brodded, pegged, stobbie, tabby, poked and pulled. Sometimes flour paste was put on the back of these mats to keep them from pulling out. Men made rug tools for their sweethearts as love tokens, often carving them from rams horn, or fashioning them from metal. Homely designs would be worked into these rag mats, such as best cow,

Cow Rug by Denise Berry-Smith in the folk art style typical of many traditional rag rugs

best sheep or family pet. Often messages such as 'Bless this House' or 'Home Sweet Home' were worked into the design – sometimes a new baby would be allowed to roll about on a new rug as a magical welcoming. In the late nineteenth century, pre-printed hessian became available, with floral designs for sale, by mail order.

Rag mats were traditionally made during the winter months. Young brides would need floor coverings when setting up home and sometimes groups of women would all work the same mat, working the pile with a bit of gossip along the way, to make mats for young couples in their village.

The newest mats were often laid out on Christmas or Easter day, first on the bed, then as a Sunday mat in the parlour. Once worn sufficiently, they would then be placed as a weekday mat in the kitchen, to then be put in the out-house, or by the back door. Finally, once completely worn out, the mat would be cut up and placed onto the compost heap.

Go through your wardrobe

Make-do and Mend

The 2nd World War initiated nearly a decade of austerity measures, during which all social classes were encouraged to reduce, reuse, recycle, or in the language of the day to 'make do and mend'. Clothes rationing was introduced in Britain in 1941 and continued long after the war ended until 1949.

Left: 1940's Poster encouraging people to 'Make-do and Mend'

THE WORLD'S FASTEST

Airlyne

HOME RUGMAKER

*THE EASY WAY
TO MAKE A
BEAUTIFUL RUG*

PRICE
28'6
COMPLETE

1950's Rug Making Kit

As Britain started to return to a state of prosperity in the 1950's, many cheap manufactured goods, including carpeting were available and affordable for the first time.

Rug with hooked centre and braided edge

Recent decades have seen a new appreciation of rag rugs as a textile art form, and while makers continue to create mats in traditional styles, many new and colourful techniques have emerged, re-inventing the craft for our eco-conscious times.

11

Tools & Equipment

Rug Hook

Rug hooks come in various sizes. I use a coarse hook that has a 2" long shank with a bulbous handle that sits comfortably in the hand. This tool enables you to pull strips of fabric up, through to the front of the hessian, that has been stretched on a frame, producing a looped pile. Very fine hooks are used for finely detailed work. When working with a rug hook you may choose to stretch your hessian on a frame or work without one.

Bodger

The bodger (also known as a spring clip) has a sprung jaw that enables you to grab tabs of fabric and pull them through hessian to work a shaggy, 'proggy' pile. You work right side up and you don't need a frame. Lots of my students have old versions of these tools.

Peg

A wooden peg is a primitive rug tool giving a shaggy 'proddy' pile. Tabs of fabric are pushed (or poked) into stretched hessian one end at a time, and caught with the other hand underneath. Sometimes known as 'pegged' or 'poked' mats, this traditional method produces the same pile as the bodger.

Latchette Hook

The latchette is used for tufting fabric tabs onto squared rug canvas. The curved hook has a flip down latchette, enabling you to pull the double ends of a short piece of folded fabric through the folded end to knot, creating a tufted stitch. This tool was used with readicut wool thrums (short pieces of rug wool) to make knotted tufted wool rugs, and you can work wool and rag in together. If you tape the latchette down, you can also use this tool to hook a looped pile.

Lots of my students already have a latchette hook, often inherited from their Mothers or Grandmothers.

Shuttle Hook

This is a two handed tool and needs both hands to operate it. Your hessian is stretched taut on an upright frame, and you work from the back, pushing the tool back and forth in a stepping motion, to create a series of even loops through to the front. This tool produces the same looped pile as a rug hook, but is quicker to use. See Celebratory Banner project in book three.

Mat, clear cutting guide, cutting gauge, scissors, cutting wheel and strip cutter

Scissors and Cutting Wheels

A pair of good dress making scissors are indispensable. Ensure that you buy a pair that fit your hand comfortably. I keep a pair of old scissors for cutting hessian and paper, and keep my dress making scissors just for cutting fabric strips and tabs.

A cutting wheel used with a self-healing mat and a clear cutting guide can allow you to cut lots of strips quickly, but watch your fingers!

Strip Cutters

There are strip cutters that can be clamped to the table edge that will cut several strips evenly with each turn of the handle. Also available are several different varieties of electric shears which may prove useful if you are working on a large project.

Cutting Gauge

A cutting gauge enables you to quickly cut lots of tabs to the same length from a long strip of fabric. The most common type of cutting gauge is a length of wood with a groove along one edge to allow the scissor blade to fit under the fabric. A strip of cardboard folded in half lengthwise will serve the same purpose.

Feverfew Cushion

Tip: After you've completed a clippy rug you can trim the ends of any long tabs to give a neat finish.

Other Tools

There are other every-day tools that may be in your house already that could be used as an alternative way to make a mat. In the past I have used flat-nosed jewellers pliers, tweezers, screwdrivers, pencils, biros, crochet hooks and wooden sticks. All these things will pull or poke tabs of fabric through your hessian, to make a proddy or hooky surface.

In addition to rug tools, the following items will be useful:

+ **For setting up a frame**
  staple gun, string, masking tape (to tape frayed edges) sewing machine optional.

+ **For marking out designs**
  chalk, magic marker, metre stick, paper to grid up your design, cardboard or newspaper to create templates.

+ **For stitching and finishing**
  Cotton carpet tape, strong thread, sack needles/strong needles, pins, carpet latex adhesive or PVA, kilt pins.

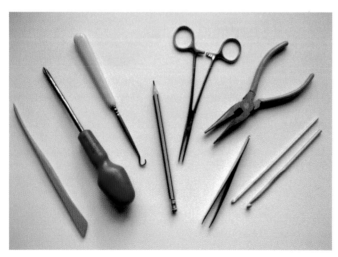

Alternative rug tools:

Sculpting tool
Screwdriver
Boot hook
Pencil
Medical clamp
Pliers
Tweezers
Crochet hooks

Frames

If you are using a bodger you will not need a frame or hoop, but for many techniques, stretching your backing on a frame can make life simpler. I tend to use a frame for any hooked project except very small pieces. If working with a shuttle hook, a frame is essential. Using a frame ensures that your backing has a taut and even tension, making it easier to push the hook in. It also enables you to see the working design in progress.

A frame is quite a simple device, so perhaps you could make one yourself. Alternatively you could use an artists stretcher, or a picture frame. If you use these you will have to tack or staple your hessian onto the frame, carefully detaching your work and repositioning it if your piece of work is larger than the frame. There are a number of commercially available frames which are simple to use.

Circular Hoops

Circular hoops used by embroiderers are ideal for small hooked projects. They have the benefit of being quick to set up and are available with or without stands. I use a 12" hoop.

Tapestry Frames

Tapestry frames and quilting frames are available in larger sizes than circular hoops, and standard models include tape covered rollers on which the backing can be stitched. Work can then be rolled on to enable you to make a larger piece. These can often be found in charity shops so can be an inexpensive way to get started.

Upright frames

I use upright frames for the majority of the rugs I make. Most upright frames are simple designs, consisting of two crossbars and two uprights that can be moved to adjust the tension on the backing. I use several frames ranging in size from 3ft square to 8ft by 6ft, but I usually work on one that is 4'6" by 3'6". These frames are larger and heavier than tapestry frames, but this weight brings its own advantage, helping to keep the frame stable in use when leant against a wall. Such a frame can be used in the horizontal position, laid over two trestles, or propped up against a table edge and your lap. As with tapestry frames, the work can be rolled onto the top crossbar, to enable you to create a larger piece

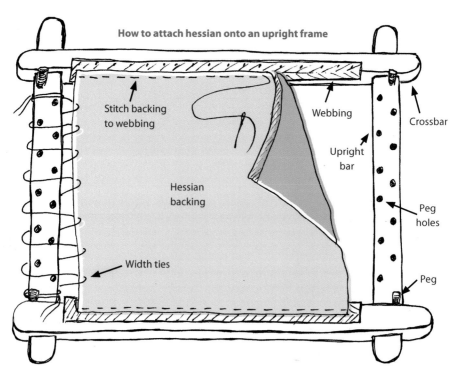

How to attach hessian onto an upright frame

Stitch backing to webbing

Webbing

Crossbar

Upright bar

Hessian backing

Peg holes

Width ties

Peg

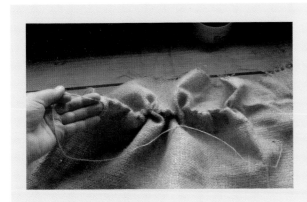

Tip: *To attach your hessian square on an upright frame, pull a thread to find the straight of the grain, and make your fold along this line.*

Treetops Vine - Work in progress on 7½ foot diameter circular rug on a large upright frame.

Silks, velvets, cottons and woollens

Textiles

Most fabrics can be used for rag rug making. Those that are most useful include woven and fine knit wool, cotton tee shirts, corduroy, sweat shirts, jogging bottoms and fleece jackets. Fun fabrics to use are lurex, nylon net, stretch velour and silks, rubber gloves, plastic bags and sheep's fleece.

Old army coats, woollen blankets, scarves and knitwear

You'll make your life easier if you avoid fabrics that are too thick, open weave or fraying, but there may be occasions when you want to use these fabrics for effect.

Tip: Charity shops will often let you search through the rag bags they keep out the back for the cloth collector, who sorts them out for use in the shoddy trade.

Source your textiles from jumble sales, boot fairs and charity shops, and use your own, and your family's cast-offs.

You may have several worn out woollies to hand, and this might decide your starting point, as tradition would have it - mats were often made with whatever was handy, worn out or available.

Cutting up your Fabrics

Before you start to cut up your fabrics into strips, its worth considering whether they are likely to fray.

Cutting through folded material

If you are using fine knit or woven woollens, you might want to run them through a hot wash to felt the fabric, locking the fibres together to keep fraying to a minimum. If you are dyeing your fabrics in a machine, this should part set the fibres.

When making a large mat, you can get large pieces of

fabric the same colour, by dyeing up old sheets or wool blankets. You can also put several different fabrics into the same dye bath for variations of the same colour.

Cutting tabs and flower petals

Start your fabric prep by turning the garment inside out and snipping away any linings, interfacings, zips and pockets. Then cut away the neckband to leave you with a flat piece of fabric. Some cottons can be ripped into strips, however this will leave a frayed raw edge, which is quicker, but not as neat as using scissors.

Cutting on the straight of the grain (usually from neck to hem) gives you a stronger working fabric strip, and makes your work more even. If cut on the bias, you may get a curved twisted edge. Fabric tends to fray more if cut on the bias.

If you are using dressmaking scissors or a cutting wheel, you can get long strips evenly by opening out a piece of fabric to lie flat, then folding over twice, and cut your strips through the layers (see image on page 21).

The thicker the fabric, the narrower the strip you will cut. Before cutting a lot of strips, it's worth testing out a strip on the hessian. Too wide and it will be difficult to pull through, too narrow, it will fall out.

If you are working with wool blanket, your strips might be ¼" (½cm) wide whereas when using fine cottons, your strips might be as wide as 1½" (4cm). However, medium weight tee shirt material which is often readily available and easy to work with, would typically be cut into strips around ⅜" (1cm).

Tip: To create a mottled 'mixy' or hit-and-miss mat, cut a whole bag of different coloured rags and pick pieces randomly. See Mixy Hearth Mat on page 8.

You can cut short tabs of fabric pieces for prodding by winding a long strip around a cutting gauge and cutting along the groove. More than two strips at a time will give you too many layers to comfortably cut through.

Be careful not to stretch the fabric strips around the cutting gauge as over-stretching will make your pieces too short. These tabs or 'clippings' were often measured round a match box in the old days.

Using a Cutting Gauge

Bloomsbury Acrobat

23

Experimenting with Fabrics

Working with different fabrics together is a way to liven up your work. What if you had for instance a beautiful red, the perfect red, but it was only thin tee shirt and not heavy enough for the project you were working on? The answer - you could bulk it up and use two pieces at once, or add a hazy overall look by combining each stitch with net. Likewise, you could use double strips of silk, thin cotton or chiffon. This is a nice way to make all sorts of materials more versatile in your work.

The fabric from old fleece jackets is quite bulky, and will splay out and cover more area with each stitch, and sit tightly in the hessian backing, so don't work your stitches too close together. The same applies to woollen blanket, tweeds, woven wool skirts, jackets and corduroy. Do try out your working widths first.

Soft woollens look great if worked in with lurex, or rubber gloves, and if you choose something beautiful that frays, you may create a pleasing effect. Velvets (if you are lucky enough to have velvet to cut up!) add a bit of glory and beautiful soft texture to cushions or seat mats.

Mistletoe Man

Four Hearts Mat

Ox Eye Daisy cushion

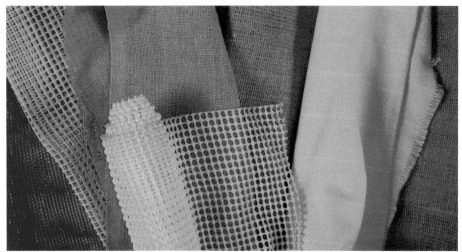

Vegetable sack, rug canvas, non-slip rubber mesh, fine hessian, monks cloth and 10oz hessian

Hessian & Backing Fabrics

Recycled hessian sacks can be washed in tepid water with a tiny bit of washing up liquid, then rinsed till the water is clear, and left to dry out in the bright sunshine. There will be an approximate shrinkage of 3" all round. If there are any moth eggs in it, this will kill them. This applies to any textile you suspect may "have the moth" – a few days in the deep freezer will also do the job!

Pre-printed hessian

Tip: *Masking tape stuck around the edges will help to prevent fraying. If you want to join your sacks to get a larger working backing, overlap your edges by at least 5" and double stitch the edges flat.*

Some of the old grain sacks had printed images on them, and were sometimes followed to save marking a pattern out.

You can unpick the jute stitching and save this thread to sew up your pieces of work when they are completed, keeping the recycling element constant.

Non-slip rubber mesh used as the base for a proggy rug

Commercially sold common 10oz jute hessian is perfectly acceptable for rag mat making. Upholstery canvas may have a stiff dressing on it, and could be soaked before use. A finer base fabric will take finely cut fabric strips. Soft cotton monks cloth is great for small projects, and open squared rug canvas is best to use when hooking cotton strips for a bath mat. Synthetic open mesh orange or green vegetable sacks can be used double, and non slip rubber mesh is ideal if you are planning to make a bath mat.

Hessian sacks

Marking Out Your Designs

If you are making a mat with straight edges, it's a good idea to mark out the perimeter lines first with chalk, using a metre stick. Brush off mistakes using an old washing up brush. Then go on to mark up your design, going over your chalk lines when you are happy with them using a magic marker.

Templates

Make your own cardboard templates out of old boxes to trace around. Simple shapes such as stars, hearts, circles and leaves can be made quickly and easily. They can be overlaid, or interchanged to create interesting cross-over shapes. Traditionally people would have used what they had to hand, like plates or cups.

Grid

If you want to create a design from a complex image, don't panic. It's not difficult to make a grid to work from.

Mark the centre vertical line on your picture, then divide the two sections in half again, so that you end up with three vertical lines. Do the same horizontally – you can continue to half each section if necessary, depending on the complexity of your design.

Copy the grid lines onto the hessian, and then copy and match up the shapes of the design in each square.

To reverse an image, hold flat against a window and trace the back, this will be your new reversed image.

Transferring a gridded design to your hessian

Winged Heart

Colour

Selecting the colours you will work with is sometimes an on-going process. I tend to start a piece of work and make decisions on colour as my piece of work progresses. For example, my mat the Winged Heart had a strong starting point as I had a much loved but worn out cherry coloured cardigan that I decided to put into a rug. The purple wings, ochre spirals and undulating blues in the sky were colours that I chose and added as the work progressed.

Working instinctively with colours you are drawn to can be a good starting point, and one which will be your own style.

Glorious colour is a sign of vitality and well being, and surrounding yourself with the colours you love is good for the soul.

If you aren't sure how far a garment will go, you can work in the strips of your first colour, and every two or three rows, introduce the second by one or two strips. Gradually increase this second colour and maybe introduce a third colour in the same way. Working this way can help bring your work to life. If for instance, you are planning a sky in your rug, (see image of Flying Crows) find several garments of similar pale blue colour and work them in, by building up your rows first in one shade, then in the next accordingly, giving visual interest and movement.

Flying Crows

The Colour Wheel

You may want to acquaint yourself with the colour wheel, as this could help you to make pleasing colour choices working on the principal that opposites on the colour wheel (known as complementary colours), if used judiciously together will enliven and bring a certain energy to your work. Sometimes it only takes a very small amount of high contrasting colour to make the statement you want.

Complementary colours if used in quantity can create a discordant effect, so be guided by your instincts and play around with the colours –

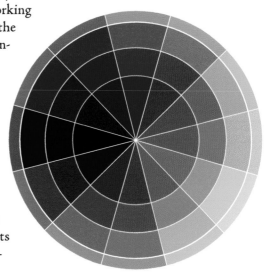

Tip: Colour Exercise

A good exercise in colour is to find a favourite postcard or photo, and pick colours from that image. That way you will find a natural series of colours. By doing this simple exercise, you can see how the colours work together, as they are in a real life composition. It will also get you away from choosing the colours you tend to always work with.

either by printing out your designs a few times to colour in different colour ways or, by laying out your coloured fabrics and moving them around until a pleasing combo is found.

The colour wheel is made up of three primary colours of red yellow and blue from which all other colours derive, producing 'warm' reds, yellows and oranges and 'cool' blues, violets and greens.

Every colour is affected by the colours that surround it. A strip of bright red placed on a purple background will look completely different if moved to a yellow background.

Your choice of colour can create dynamic contrasts or harmonious blends. Learn to trust your own colour sense to find the colours that work for you.

Inspiration

Allium Rug

All sorts of things inspire my work. I love the endless possibilities of colour combinations, and I love nature and the natural world. My inspiration folders are full of postcards I've collected, sketches, pictures from magazines, leaves and pressed flowers. I take digital images of seed heads and pods, and beautiful garden flowers, earth and sky landscapes and many other things, I see when travelling.

I love old symbols, Celtic and Medieval art work. I collect shells, stones and old buttons. I look closely at tree bark for pattern and colour. Hazel bark is wonderfully speckled!

Umbellifer plant design marked out

Every now and then I might come across a piece of fabric in a beautiful colour or texture, and keep these swatches on my pin board. I collect coloured darning and knitting yarns when I can find them in charity shops to use when embellishing my work.

If you have not done so already, it's a good plan to make up your own inspirational folders, and collect postcards, pictures and take photographs of anything you see that inspires you creatively. Keeping a record like this will be an on-going inspiration and will remind you of when you were first inspired.

About the Author

I began making rag rugs after learning rudimentary weaving in 1990. I have always loved collecting old textiles, and I was looking for a way to use them in my work as an artist. I came across some old rag rug hand tools, and my journey began.

I have worked professionally as a designer, maker, teacher and writer for the past 20 years, specialising in rag rug making. Recycling and sustainability are important to me and with my project 'Creativity in Schools', I have brought these fun traditional techniques to school children, to raise some 'eco' awareness in the next generation. I also teach rag rug making and felt making to adults at various venues across the UK and hold my own regular workshops in East Sussex.

My work was commissioned by the Tate Gallery shop in London to accompany an exhibition of work by the Bloomsbury group, the literary and art group of the 1920's. I was subsequently commissioned to make a reproduction of an original Bloomsbury rag rug for Charleston, home of the Bloomsbury group Nr. Firle, East Sussex, England.

I am also a felt maker and make seamless jackets and clothing. I work to commission and sell at art shows, in galleries and I open my studio to the public usually for one month each year

My work has been exhibited in National Trust venues, and has featured in the Sunday Times and Sunday Telegraph. I have also appeared on BBC and Channel 4 television with my work.

www.debbiesiniska.co.uk